THE
PERIOD
BOOK.

T0022726

Also by Karen Gravelle

What's Going on Down There?
A Boy's Guide to Growing Up

The Driving Book

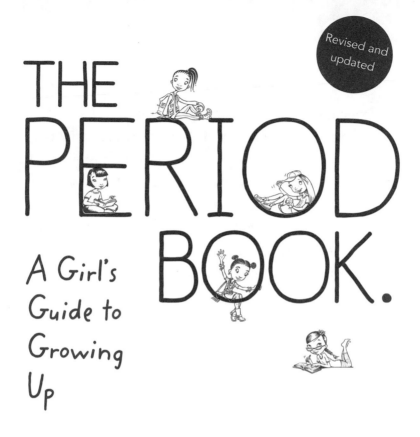

THE PERIOD BOOK.

A Girl's Guide to Growing Up

Karen Gravelle with Jennifer Gravelle Stratton
illustrated by **Debbie Palen**

Revised and updated

BLOOMSBURY
NEW YORK LONDON OXFORD NEW DELHI SYDNEY

ACKNOWLEDGMENTS

Since it's been a long time since we were young, we wanted to find out what questions and concerns today's 8- to 12-year-old girls have about puberty. So we decided to ask some girls your age. Are we glad we did! Their questions, comments, and suggestions made this a much better book, and we want to say, "Thank you for your help!" to all of them, but especially to Alexandra, Samantha, Marianne, Jenna, and Katherine.

Copyright © 1996 and 2017 by Karen Gravelle
Illustrations copyright © 1996 and 2017 by Debbie Palen
All rights reserved. No part of this book may be reproduced or transmitted in any form
or by any means, electronic or mechanical, including photocopying, recording, or by any
information storage and retrieval system, without permission in writing from the publisher.

Original edition published in the United States of America in 1996
by Walker Books for Young Readers, an imprint of Bloomsbury Publishing, Inc.
Revised edition published in the United States of America in June 2017
by Bloomsbury Children's Books
www.bloomsbury.com

Bloomsbury is a registered trademark of Bloomsbury Publishing Plc

For information about permission to reproduce selections from this book, write to
Permissions, Bloomsbury Children's Books, 1385 Broadway, New York, New York 10018
Bloomsbury books may be purchased for business or promotional use. For information on bulk
purchases please contact Macmillan Corporate and Premium Sales Department at
specialmarkets@macmillan.com

LCCN of original edition: 95031101
ISBN 978-1-61963-662-0 (paperback)

Book design by Yelena Safronova
Printed and bound in the U.S.A. by LSC Communications, Crawfordsville, IN
15 17 19 20 18 16

CONTENTS

A NOTE FROM JENNIFER

Although Jennifer is married now with a family of her own, she still agrees with what she had to say when she was fifteen.

When my aunt Karen Gravelle asked me to help her with this book, I agreed immediately. I think the more books on the market about getting your period, the better. The only other way you can learn about this subject is from your mother or in school. I was lucky, because my mom and I could talk about the topic. I know that for most girls, it's pretty embarrassing to talk in public about getting your period. Many girls think they'll look stupid if they don't know something, so they can be afraid to ask questions—particularly if the question sounds kind of dumb, like, *What happens if you can't get a tampon out?*

My aunt and I wanted to answer questions that girls my age would like to ask but are afraid to. Chapter 7, "What If . . . ?", is my favorite part of the book. These are the sort of things you want to know about but probably won't bring up in a class.

We also hope that this book will help parents and daughters talk about menstruation and sex. I know a lot of girls have trouble discussing these topics with their parents. I'd just like to say to parents that you shouldn't think about it as the Talk. Think of it as a conversation that you may have with your daughter again and again. There's never a good time for the Talk, but there's always time for a conversation.

Jennifer
(age fifteen)

INTRODUCTION

As you can tell from the title, this book is about getting your period—what a period is, why it happens, what it feels like, and what to do when you get it. But it's way more than that! This book is really about changes, since the reason a girl gets her period in the first place is that her body is changing from a child's body into a woman's body. The time when these changes happen is called puberty. Are you between eight and eleven years old, give or take a little? If so, then chances are you've already started to go through puberty. If not, you probably will soon.

It's a funny thing, but most of us aren't totally thrilled with changes, even when they are something we really want. The problem is that we often don't have much say over when they happen. It can be hard when things change before we're ready for them to change—or after we've been ready for ages! This is especially true when the change is an important one, like starting middle school. It's even more true when what's changing is your own body.

Not sure how you feel about all this happening to you? Well, you're not alone! Some girls can hardly wait for their bodies to change, while others would be very happy to wait a little longer. Many girls feel one way on some days and just the opposite on others.

Although you can't control when these changes will happen to you, knowing what to expect helps to make things easier. This book will tell you what to expect not only with your period but with all the other changes going on in your body. Some of these changes you may have already noticed, so let's start with them.

∞ 1 ∞

CHANGES OF PUBERTY
Those You Can See

If you look at a classroom of sixth or seventh graders, you'll notice something strange. When they were in the third grade, these boys and girls were pretty much the same height. But now that they're eleven or twelve years old, the girls are generally taller than the boys. What's going on?

THE GROWTH SPURT

The answer is that many of these sixth-grade girls have started their growth spurts. The growth spurt is one of the first signs of puberty—and one you can't help but notice! When boys and girls are younger, they grow at pretty much the same rate. That is, they both get about two inches taller each year. But when girls enter puberty, they start growing much faster, sometimes as much as four inches a year.

Of course, boys go through puberty too in order to become men. But they generally don't start their growth spurts until they are a little older. So for a few years, most girls are taller than the boys. When boys finally start growing, in their mid to late teens, they usually grow taller than the girls.

Besides getting taller, a girl's arms, legs, and feet also begin growing much faster. In fact, feet are likely to grow the fastest of all. For some girls, seeing their feet getting bigger and bigger can be scary. It may seem as if their feet are growing out of control and that they will end up with huge feet or feet way too long for the rest of their body. Fortunately, this doesn't happen.

Although your feet grow the fastest, they also stop growing first. So, when you get taller, your feet will be the right size for someone of your height.

CHANGING SHAPE (BREASTS!)

Besides getting taller and longer, your body is growing in other directions as well. When you enter puberty, your hips and thighs begin to become wider and more curvy. But the most obvious change is that you're beginning to develop breasts. For many girls, this is the first sign of puberty.

As you know, the chests of little kids all look the same. In both boys and girls, breasts are flat except for a small, slightly raised circle in the center of each called a nipple. Sometime between the ages of eight and eleven (give or take a little), your breasts will begin to swell and grow out from your chest. This happens because you're developing milk glands that will make it possible for you to nurse a baby later on. Fat develops around these

glands to protect them, which gives your breasts their adult shape.

This doesn't happen all at once, of course. At first, only the area around the nipple begins to stick out. The nipple feels harder and is sometimes a little tender. The nipple and the ring around it also become larger and darker in color. Often, one breast starts growing before the other. If you don't know that this is perfectly normal, having one breast that's growing when the other isn't can be frightening! Does this mean that something has gone very wrong and you're going to be the only girl in the world with just one breast? Don't panic! The other breast will start growing soon. In a little while it will catch up with the breast that started growing first.

WHEN WILL MINE START TO DEVELOP?

Are you wondering when your breasts will start to appear? Although most girls are between eight and eleven when this happens, some are a little younger and some are a little older when their breasts first begin to grow. Girls whose breasts start developing when they are eight or nine often don't feel ready yet and aren't too happy about this. On the other hand, girls who don't start developing until long after their friends have started frequently feel left out. It helps to know that by

age fifteen or sixteen, you and all your friends will have gotten your breasts.

By the way, you might think that girls whose breasts begin developing at a younger age will have bigger breasts than girls whose breasts don't start growing until they are older. Actually, when you start to develop breasts has nothing to do with how big your breasts will eventually become.

Breasts are a very big deal in American culture, and something people pay a lot of attention to. Since they are an obvious sign to everyone that a young girl is growing up, many girls feel proud when their breasts start to develop. Sometimes girls whose breasts haven't started to grow are a little envious of those who already have them and wish that their own would hurry up and appear.

On the other hand, all the attention paid to breasts makes other girls feel self-conscious when their breasts begin to develop. Every now and then it seems that the whole world is staring at their chests. A lot of girls have both feelings—happy they are getting breasts but a little uncomfortable that they're so noticeable.

Besides feeling self-conscious about the fact that they are developing breasts, girls often worry whether their breasts are the "right" size or whether they look okay. Even if they like their breasts, they may think their hips or some other part of their bodies have become too big or perhaps not big enough. Deciding for some reason that their bodies aren't perfect can make them feel unattractive and unhappy.

Does this sound like the way you feel? If so, try to remember that just as different colors of hair, skin, and eyes are all pretty, different body shapes are attractive too. The truth is that there isn't a "perfect" type of breasts or hips or waist that you should have, any more than there is a perfect eye color.

WHAT ABOUT BRAS?

Now that you're developing breasts, does that mean you need to start wearing a bra? Well, that depends on you and whether you want to or not. There are lots of good reasons for choosing to wear a bra, no matter what size your breasts are. Some girls just like the feeling that they're growing up, and wearing a bra is part of that. Others don't like having their nipples show through their clothes, and a bra takes care of that problem. A lot of girls just feel more comfortable wearing a bra. It gives their breasts support and keeps their breasts from bouncing up and down. Bras also help to protect your breasts, particularly when you're playing sports.

There are good reasons not to wear a bra too. You may not think that you need one because your breasts are still small. Since your breasts don't jiggle anyway, you don't feel they need extra support. And bras aren't the only way to keep your nipples from showing through

your clothes. Wearing a T-shirt or tank top under your clothes works just as well. Maybe you just don't feel ready to wear a bra, even if you have bigger breasts, and that's reason enough not to. In fact, you don't need a good reason not to wear a bra. After all, your breasts aren't going to fall off without one. So, do what seems right for you—and feel free to change your mind at any time.

If you do decide you want to wear a bra, though, you'll have a lot to choose from. Many bras are meant more for adults, like strapless bras, so let's just talk about the ones that might be right for you.

CAMIS

A cami (which is short for *camisole*) looks a little like a sleeveless undershirt, only it has thin straps and is made of satin, nylon, or soft cotton and has a built-in shelf bra. Camis look great under a shirt and are really comfortable.

TRAINERS

Trainers, or training bras, are really comfortable too. These bras are made of a stretchy fabric so you can

pull them over your head. Like camis, they don't provide much support, because they are intended for girls whose breasts are just beginning to grow. (By the way, training bras don't train your breasts to do anything. They're kind of like training wheels on a bike—they're a first step in wearing a bra.)

SOFT-CUP BRAS

Soft-cup bras are the next step up from a training bra and give you a little more support.

SHAPED CUP OR PADDED BRAS

Padded bras have some padding sewn into the cups to help shape your breasts. (They also make your breasts look bigger.)

UNDERWIRE BRAS

Underwire bras have curved wires sewn around the bottom of each cup to give extra support, so girls with larger breasts often like these bras—but so do a lot of girls with smaller breasts.

SPORTS BRAS

 Sports bras are designed to keep your boobs from bouncing around when you are doing things like jogging or playing sports. But they're popular with girls who aren't very active too. Sports bras are very comfortable, and a lot of girls like the way they look. There are sports bras for all breast sizes.

CROP TOP BRAS

Crop top bras resemble sports bras, but don't give you as much support. Some also come in cooler styles and fabrics than sports bras. They come in lots of sizes too.

To put on camis, trainers, sports bras, and crop top bras, you just pull them over your head. With soft-cup bras, padded bras, and underwire bras, you slip your arms through the straps and close the bra with hooks that are in the front or the back.

Figuring Out Your Bra Size

Most bras have a size that is made up of two parts, a number and a letter. What do they mean and how do you figure out what size is yours?

1. The number—or band size—is easy. You find your band size by taking a tape measure and measuring around your back right under your breasts. Then add 5 to that number, and you have your band size (round up if you get an odd number, because band sizes come only in even numbers). For example, if you are 24 inches around when you measure yourself, you add 5 and get 29. Then your band size is 30.

2. The letters are your cup size, or the size of your breasts themselves. They go from the smallest, which is AAA, to the largest, which is generally D. (There are larger cup sizes than D for women with bigger breasts, but girls your age whose breasts are just developing are unlikely to need them.) To find your cup size, first measure around your back and

over your breasts at the nipple. (Be careful not to pull the tape too tight. It should rest against your breasts without squishing them.) Now subtract the inches you used to find your band size from this measurement. In other words, if you measured 25 inches under your breasts and 26 inches over your breasts, then 26 - 25 = 1. The difference—in this case, 1—lets you know that your cup size is an A.

Different Cup Sizes

Less Than 1"	AAA, AA
1"	A
2"	B
3"	C
4"	D

3. If you have trouble measuring yourself or figuring out your bra size, you can always ask your mom or another female relative or friend

you trust to help you. Also, most department stores have saleswomen who are used to helping customers determine the size that is right for them.

4. Of course, you can always just try on a couple of sizes to see which fits best. If your breasts have just started to develop, you are probably a triple A (AAA) or double A (AA). Is the bra too small? Then try an A. If your breasts are on the large side, try a B or maybe a C. Too big? Then try the next cup size down.

5. Does the bra feel comfortable? Does it give you enough support? Do you like the way it looks? If the answers are all "yes," then it's the right bra for you!

Important tip: always try on a bra before buying it!

Two bras that are exactly the same band and cup size but different styles can fit you very differently. This is why it's not a good idea to buy a bra online unless you're okay with having to send it back, especially if you're just starting out and your breasts are still growing.

Matching Your Bra to Your Boobs

Some bras can be worn by anyone, while others are better for girls with breasts of a certain size. This chart will give you an idea of which you may like best. But remember, the important thing is whether the bra is comfortable and you like it—not whether the type of bra matches your breast size below.

If Your Boobs Are This Size, Then You'll Probably Like:

Size AAA/AA	camis, trainers, and crop top bras
Size AA/A	camis, soft-cup bras, crop top bras, and sports bras
Size A	soft-cup bras, shaped-cup bras, sports bras, and crop top bras
Size B	shaped-cup bras, sports bras, and some crop top bras

| Size C | shaped-cup bras, underwire bras, and sports bras |
| Size D | underwire bras, sports bras |

P.S. Whether you want to wear a padded bra or not depends more on whether you want your boobs to look fuller or more shapely than it does on what size your breasts actually are. Since your breasts are probably the right size for someone with your body type, you don't need to wear a padded bra unless you want to.

GETTING USED TO A NEW BODY

There's no question that a different body can take some getting used to. After years of being flat in front and behind, it can seem to some girls that their new hips and breasts make them look fat. It doesn't help that the longer, heavier bones and muscles that come with the growth spurt mean more pounds. So, when these girls step on a scale, they're convinced that they're *really* overweight.

But think about it—you can't very well get taller and

still weigh the same as before. So,
these extra pounds don't mean that
you are fat. (We'll talk more about
the right weight for you in Chapter
9.) And give yourself some time to
get used to your new breasts, hips,
and butt before you decide if
they make you look too big.
To your surprise, you may
end up thinking you actually
like the way they look.

The shape of your body isn't the only thing you may
have trouble getting used to. Longer legs and bigger
feet may not always do exactly what you want them
to do, especially if you've grown a lot recently. It can
take a while for your brain to learn how to get your new
arms, legs, and feet to work together. So, if it seems
like you've become really clumsy lately or you're not
as good at sports as you used to be, give yourself a
break. Luckily, this awkward period won't last long, and
pretty soon these parts of your body will start working
together again.

Not too happy with all the changes of puberty? It might
help you to know that many girls aren't completely
crazy about them either—at least not all the time. Just

remember: although it may take a while to get used to these changes, most girls feel pretty good about them in the end.

Here is the way some girls are feeling about these changes, at least right now. What about you?

"Even if you know what's happening about getting your first period, it's a little scary. But not much."

*"Before I started getting breasts, I was really good at soccer. But the last time I blocked the ball off my chest, it really **hurt**! Now I'm kind of afraid to do that."*

"I like teenage styles, so it's good that I'm getting breasts. The clothes fit me better now."

*"I thought the growth spurt was supposed to make you taller, but all it's doing is making me **wider**. I have these big boobs and my butt is **gi-normous**! I look like a bowling ball. I **hate** this!"*

"Before, my friends were all developing and I wasn't. I was really worried that something was wrong with me. But now I know that developing later is not a problem, so I'm okay with it."

"I kind of like getting boobs. It makes me feel more confident to know I'm developing."

*"I've always been skinny. But I grew a lot last year and now I'm skinny and **really** tall. I look like a giant freak when I'm hanging out with my friends, who are all shorter and have boobs and everything. But the other day, a friend of my mother's who's a clothing designer told me, 'You have the perfect face and body for high fashion. In a couple of years, you should think about becoming a model.' I felt a whole lot better about the way I looked after that!"*

"I'm developing much faster than my best friend. But we talk about it. Nothing comes between us— we're still best friends."

*"It seems like there's **so much** to worry about now—nipples showing through my clothes, getting my first period away from home, looking good, wearing the right clothes, keeping up my grades."*

HAIR IN NEW PLACES

For other girls, the first sign of puberty is that they begin to grow hair in new places. One of these places is the pubic area, the place on your lower torso between your legs. During childhood, this area is hairless or has very light, unnoticeable hairs. Sometime between the ages of eight and eleven, however, a different kind of hair begins to appear here.

The growth of pubic hair starts very slowly—only one or two hairs at first. It's easy to tell these new hairs from childhood hairs because they are darker, longer, and curlier. Over time, more of these hairs appear, covering your pubic area in a kind of upside-down triangle.

If you are a blonde or a redhead, you may find to

your surprise that you have much darker pubic hair. And even if the color of your pubic hair is similar to the color of the hair on your head, it may have a very different texture. For example, girls who have straight hair on their head generally have curlier hair in their pubic area.

Along with pubic hair, hair begins to grow in the armpits. The hair on your legs and sometimes on your arms may become darker too. You may even notice darker hairs on your upper lip as well.

TO SHAVE OR NOT TO SHAVE?

You've been noticing that the hair on your legs and under your arms has gotten thicker and darker. Should you shave it off? Again, that depends on you. First, ask yourself why you want to shave. Is it because you think this is something you're supposed to do? Or maybe your friends think that this hair looks gross and that everyone—including you—should get rid of it. Some girls shave under their arms but are okay with the hair on their legs—or vice versa. How do you feel?

People's opinions about women and girls shaving are one of those things that vary across different cultures. In some places, hair on the legs and armpits of females is seen as perfectly okay. In other places, people tend to find smooth, hairless legs and underarms on girls more attractive and more feminine. But what matters is what *you* think.

If You've Decided to Shave, Now What?

1. Make sure your parents are okay with your decision.

2. Decide how you want to remove the hair. Shaving with a razor isn't the only way. There are waxes and creams that you can use instead, but they can irritate your skin. Most girls find a razor the safest and easiest way, so let's concentrate on that.

3. Choose the kind of razor you want to use. Although there are gazillions of different razors to choose from, they tend to fall into two types—throwaway ones and refillable razors. You'll probably like the throwaway ones better, as they're more convenient and you're less likely to cut yourself trying to replace the blade.

4. Hair is easier to cut when it's soft and wet, so many girls shave their legs and underarms when they are taking a bath or a shower. You'll want to use warm water and soap, shaving cream, or hair conditioner on the places you wish to shave. This softens the hair and helps the razor to slide smoothly over your skin.

Many razors come with moisturizers already included.

5. *Go slowly and gently!* It doesn't take much pressure to shave, so just let the blade slide lightly over your skin. When shaving your legs, start at the ankle and go up. Be really careful around your anklebone, your shin, and your knee, as these are the places you're most likely to nick yourself.

6. Rinse the razor blade often while you are shaving and after you're finished to keep it from getting clogged with hair and soap or shaving cream. Even if you're careful to keep your razor clean, however, the blade will become dull after four or five uses, so you'll need change it for a new one then.

7. Wait about five minutes after shaving your underarms before putting on deodorant. Your skin is especially sensitive after shaving, and the deodorant can irritate it.

8. It is never a good idea to share a razor with someone else, even a good friend or

a family member, since this is one way to spread germs.

SKIN CHANGES

PIMPLES

Some of the changes you probably wish weren't so easy to see are the ones that pop up on your skin. After a whole lifetime of never having to think about your skin, suddenly there you are, checking your face daily for (ick!) *pimples.* For both boys and girls, pimples are a sign of puberty that they could happily do without. Although a few girls are lucky enough never to have this problem, most girls' skin breaks out at least occasionally.

How come? The answer is that your oil glands have started to speed up production. During puberty, the oil glands in the skin begin to produce greater amounts of oil. When this oil clogs a pore in your skin, it causes a blackhead or a whitehead. If the clogged pore gets inflamed, a pimple results.

If you wonder why some girls break out more than others do, part of the answer may have to do with their skin type. Some girls have naturally oilier skin, while other girls' skin is drier. Many girls have combination skin, with oilier patches in some places and drier skin in other spots. Not surprisingly, pimples are more likely to pop up in the oilier places.

There isn't anything you can do to keep your oil glands from producing more oil, but there are things you can do to keep your pores from getting clogged. The most important one is to keep your face and hair clean. (You'll find a lot more tips on handling pimples in Chapter 6.)

PERSPIRATION

Oil glands aren't the only glands that become more active at this time—sweat glands also crank up production. Not only do girls (and boys) who have entered puberty sweat more than they did when they were children, but their sweat begins to have a different smell. Why is that?

The answer is that this new sweat is coming from sweat glands in your armpits, between your legs, and on your feet—places that are damp and don't get much air, exactly the places that germs love. As these germs grow in your sweat, they give off stinky chemicals, resulting in some less-than-lovely BO, or body odor.

Before you let this gross you out, remember—BO is pretty easy to deal with. Most of the time, just bathing every day and wearing clean clothes is enough to keep smelly perspiration in check. If not, you may also want to use an underarm deodorant or an antiperspirant. A deodorant gets rid of odors, while an antiperspirant also stops perspiration.

THE PRIVATE YOU

The reproductive, or sex, organs are the parts of the body that make it possible for a girl or woman to have a baby. They are the organs that make girls different from boys. Most people refer to the sex organs inside the body as the internal reproductive organs. Those on the outside are commonly called the genitals, or your private parts. As you can guess, puberty means some big changes happen here.

Although your genitals are certainly visible, many

girls have never had a chance to look at them. It's surprising, but girls who have helped to take care of their little brothers often know much more about what a boy's genitals look like than their own.

The best way to find out what your genitals are like is to take a look for yourself. And the easiest way to do that is to hold a mirror between your legs. If this seems like a strange thing to do, it's probably because we're taught that this is a private area that should be kept covered. But that means private from other people— not yourself! After all, a boy's genitals are private too, but no one thinks it's weird when he looks at them.

If you lie on your back with a mirror between your

legs, this is what you'll see. At the top is the area where your pubic hairs first begin to grow. You're probably already familiar with this part of your body because you can see it without a mirror. During puberty, this area develops a pad of fat under the skin that makes it look a little more rounded than before.

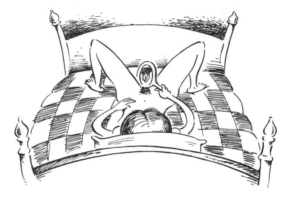

Moving down, you'll see two folds, or flaps, of skin, one on each side of a narrow separation. These are called the outer lips. If you've entered puberty, you may notice that pubic hairs have started to grow here as well. The outer lips of a little girl are small, smooth, and often don't touch each other. But as you enter puberty, these lips become fuller and grow closer together. This is to provide protection for the more delicate area underneath. The outer lips also become darker and sort of wrinkled.

If you look inside the outer lips, you'll see another

set of lips. As you've probably guessed, these are called the inner lips. In young girls, the inner lips are small and not very noticeable, but in puberty, they begin to grow rapidly. The inner lips may actually grow bigger than the outer lips and stick out from between the outer lips. Different girls develop differently shaped inner lips. But whatever kind you have, they will be darker and more wrinkled than the inner lips you had as a child.

Now separate the inner lips. There are three very important organs protected beneath. At the bottom is an opening that leads inside your body. This is the entrance to your vagina, which we'll talk more about in the next chapter. If you are still fairly young, the entrance to your vagina may be hard to see, since it isn't very big yet, but the drawing on this page will give you an idea of where to look.

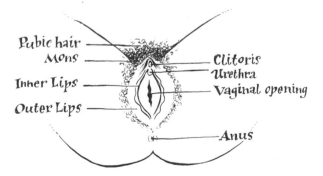

Right above the entrance to your vagina is another,

much smaller opening. This is your urethra, the opening though which you urinate, or pee. This isn't a sexual organ, but it's good to know about it just the same.

At the top, where your inner lips join, is your clitoris. Unlike the entrance to your vagina or your urethra, your clitoris is not an opening. Instead, it's a little button-like bulge. The clitoris is very sensitive and results in pleasurable, sexy feelings when touched.

Finally, while you've got your mirror out, take a look at the large opening at the very bottom of your body where the two sides of your behind come together. This is your anus, the place where bowel movements, or poop, come out of your body. Like your urethra, it's not a sexual organ, so it's not part of your genitals.

Your vaginal opening leads to your internal sex organs, which have also been changing as you've entered puberty. Let's talk about these changes next.

∼ 2 ∽

CHANGES OF PUBERTY
Those You Can't See

Big changes are going on inside your body too! Like other parts of your body, your internal reproductive organs are growing and developing. Of course, you can't see these changes without some help. But the picture on page 34 will give you a good idea of what your internal reproductive organs look like and what's going on there. This is what you would see if you could look inside yourself with X-ray vision.

OVARIES

Do you see the two roundish organs on either side? These are your ovaries, and they contain the eggs from which babies grow. There are hundreds of thousands of eggs in your ovaries, and they've been

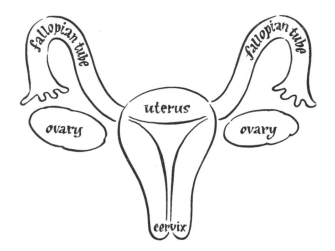

there since the day you were born. As you can guess, the eggs must be very tiny if they are all going to fit inside. In fact, one egg is about the size of the tip of a needle.

The eggs don't begin to mature until you reach puberty, so they can't grow into a baby until then. Of course, it will be a while before you are ready to have children. So don't worry—just because your eggs *can* become babies when you reach puberty doesn't mean they will right now. As you probably know, it takes both sperm from a man and an egg from a woman to make a baby, and they have to have sex in order for the two to join. You're a long way away from that!

You're probably wondering what in the world you would do with hundreds of thousands of eggs, since you certainly don't plan to have that many children! Only eight or nine hundred of these eggs will ever mature, and only very few of those will ever become babies. So, no matter how many children you plan to have, you'll have more than enough eggs.

FALLOPIAN TUBES

Your fallopian tubes are easy to spot—in the drawing, they look a little like two long arms with fingers at the ends reaching out toward your ovaries. The job of the fallopian tubes is to guide the egg to the uterus (the next organ we'll talk about).

The "fingers" at the ends of the fallopian tubes are actually more like fringe. This fringe is very important in helping an egg find its way across the space from the ovary to the tube. By waving back and forth, the fringe sweeps the egg toward the entrance to the tube.

The fallopian tubes are also a lot smaller than you might think. When you're an adult, they will be about four inches long but only as thick as a strand of spaghetti.

UTERUS

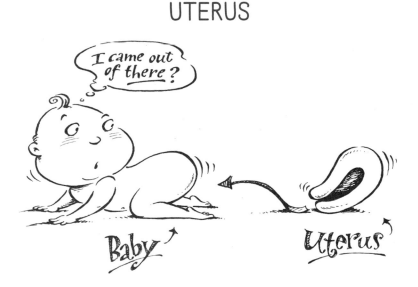

Your uterus is the large triangular organ between the fallopian tubes. The uterus is also called the womb, and it's the place where an egg develops into a baby. The size of the uterus will really surprise you. Even when you're full-grown, your uterus will be only about the size of a fist. If you are wondering how a baby could possibly fit in such a small place, the answer is simple—the uterus is very elastic. As the baby grows, the uterus stretches to make room for it. You've seen pregnant women, so you have a pretty good idea of how far it can stretch.

CERVIX

At the bottom of the uterus is your cervix, a knob of flesh with a small hole in the center. The purpose of the cervix is to protect the inside of your uterus. The little hole in the middle of the cervix is to provide an opening between the uterus and the vagina. When it needs to—as when a baby is being born—the little hole opens wide.

VAGINA

Your vagina is the passageway in and out of your reproductive system. There is a protective strip of skin stretched at least partly across the vaginal opening to the outside. This skin is called a hymen, and it has a hole (or even several holes) in it. Like your uterus, your vagina is *very* elastic. Most of the time, the sides of the vagina lie touching each other. But during birth, the vagina stretches a lot to let the baby pass through. Your vagina grows larger as you go from childhood to adulthood. By the time you are an adult, it will be three to five inches long.

Some Hymen Variations

Your vagina has its own special fluid that helps to keep it clean and elastic. This fluid, or discharge, is clear, milky white, or yellowish and can be either slippery or somewhat sticky. The fluid flushes out dead cells that your vagina has shed and keeps your vagina moist so that it can stretch. Vaginal discharge is the reason for the yellow stain that begins to appear on your underpants. This discharge may have a slight odor, but the smell is not unpleasant. All this is perfectly normal and a sign that your body is maturing.

Besides growing, your reproductive organs shift position a little as you go from being a child to an adult. These shifts are easiest to see when you look at the body from the side, as in the pictures on page 39.

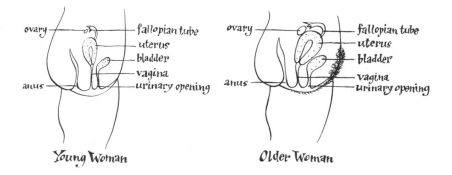

ovary — fallopian tube, uterus, bladder, vagina, urinary opening — anus

Young Woman

ovary — fallopian tube, uterus, bladder, vagina, urinary opening — anus

Older Woman

The biggest change is in the position of your uterus. In a girl, the uterus is positioned straight up and down. But by the time most girls have grown into women, the uterus tilts toward the front of the body. Since the bottoms of the fallopian tubes are attached to the uterus, they tilt in that direction too.

Not everyone's uterus tilts forward, though. In some women, it remains in a straight position, and in others, it tips backward. These positions are perfectly normal, although not as common as a forward tilt.

Of course, you don't have X-ray eyes, so you can't see the changes

Straight   Backward Tilt   Forward Tilt

happening inside your body. But when your reproductive organs have developed enough for you to have a baby, you'll get a very definite sign—you'll have your first period.

∽ 3 ∾

YOUR PERIOD

Your period is the only sign that you will see of an invisible cycle that goes on inside the bodies of all women. This cycle starts about once a month, when one of your eggs matures and leaves the ovary. If you remember, the egg is then swept into one of the fallopian tubes and is on its way to your uterus.

Meanwhile, the uterus has been busy preparing for this. The lining of the uterus develops a thick spongy cushion to give the egg a safe, nourishing place to grow into a baby. By the time an egg enters the uterus, everything is ready for it to settle in. If the woman is going to have a baby, the egg attaches to the lining, starts to develop, and a pregnancy begins.

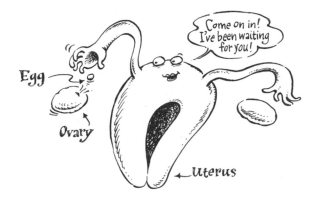

Most of the time, though, the woman isn't going to have a baby, so the egg doesn't attach to the lining. After a day or so, the egg just disintegrates and disappears.

What happens to the nice thick lining of the uterus in that case? Since there's no need for it right now, the uterus just gets rid of it. The blood-filled lining begins to shed slowly, dribbling out of your vagina for the next two to seven or eight days. The time when you are bleeding is called a menstrual period, menstruation, or just a period, for short.

While you are busy having your period, your ovary (this time the one on the opposite side) is getting another egg ready to go. About a month after the previous egg was released, another mature egg will pop into the space between the ovary and one of the fallopian tubes, and the cycle starts all over again. This cycle takes place approximately every month from a girl's first period until she reaches her forties or fifties. Then her ovaries begin to produce mature eggs less frequently until they stop producing altogether. At that point, she is no longer able to have children.

WHEN WILL I GET *MY* FIRST PERIOD?

That's hard to say. In the same way that different girls begin to develop breasts and pubic hair at different ages, there are also differences in when girls get their first period. A girl can get her first period when she is as young as eight or nine or not until she's sixteen or even seventeen. Most girls start somewhere between the ages of eleven and thirteen. But that says nothing about *you*.

One way of getting some idea of when you're likely to get your first period is to look at your body. Have you begun to develop breasts or pubic hair? Regardless of your age, your period won't start until after you've noticed these changes. If neither of these has happened to you yet, you probably have a while to go before you can expect your first period. Have you begun to have some vaginal discharge? Most girls begin to notice this discharge a year or two before they have their first period, so this will give you another clue.

HOW LONG WILL MY PERIOD LAST?

It's also not possible to predict how many days your period will last, or how much you will actually bleed. Some girls have periods that last only two or three days, while others have periods that last up to seven or eight days. Some girls bleed only a little, while others bleed more heavily. Lots of times, a girl will have a shorter, lighter period one month and a longer, heavier period the next. This is especially true when you first start having your period, before your body has had a chance to settle into a regular routine.

Although periods come about once a month, that can mean every twenty-six days for some girls and every thirty-two days for others. If you're like most girls, you'll probably get your period about every twenty-eight days. Don't expect to be that regular when you first start, however. For the first couple of years, you may have two periods with only a week in between and then not have another one for several months. In fact, you may never be very regular—that's normal for some girls too.

KEEPING TRACK

The best way to learn about your own special cycle is to keep track of your periods on a calendar or a chart. Now there's even an app for your phone that you can use for this. Start with the first day of your period, and mark the days that you have bleeding. If you want, you can also make notes about which day has the heaviest flow, how you are feeling at the time, or whatever you'd like to remember. If you keep a record of your next twelve periods or so, you'll begin to see a pattern. This pattern will help you know how often to expect your period, how long your periods are likely to be, and which days to be sure to carry extra pads or tampons. (We'll talk more about what to wear when you have your period in Chapter 4.)

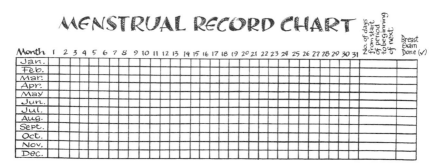

MENSTRUAL RECORD CHART

Month	1	2	3	4	5	6	7	8	9	10	11	12	13	14	15	16	17	18	19	20	21	22	23	24	25	26	27	28	29	30	31	No. of days from start of period to beginning of next	Breast Exam Done (✓)
Jan.																																	
Feb.																																	
Mar.																																	
Apr.																																	
May																																	
Jun.																																	
Jul.																																	
Aug.																																	
Sept.																																	
Oct.																																	
Nov.																																	
Dec.																																	

TYPE OF FLOW:

Normal   ☒
Exceptionally light   ⊡
Exceptionally heavy   ■
Spotting   Ⓢ

WHAT DOES A PERIOD FEEL LIKE?

There are probably as many answers to that question as there are girls on the planet. Not only do different girls feel differently, but the same girl can very differently from one month to the next. Some girls feel nothing unusual either before or during their periods. In a lot of ways, these girls are lucky. But since they don't get any signs that their periods are on the way, they have to be especially careful to keep track of when their next period is due to begin, or they'll be caught by surprise when it comes.

ADVANCE SIGNALS

Most girls, however, get signals from their bodies telling them that a period is on the way. The most common clue that your period will start in a few days is that your breasts may feel a little more swollen or tender than usual. You may also feel a little bloated or have some lower-back pain.

Some girls notice that they feel more emotional right before and at the beginning of their periods. This can mean that they are a little cranky or get upset by things that usually wouldn't bother them.

Often, girls may notice that their skin is more likely

to break out at the beginning of their periods, so this can be another tip. All these advance signals tend to weaken, become less noticeable, or disappear when your period actually starts.

CRAMPS

Cramps are a pain or an ache in your abdomen that can come with your period. Most girls have cramps at least once in their life, and others have them often. Cramps are caused by the muscles in your uterus contracting and, although they are uncomfortable, they don't mean anything is wrong. Cramps usually occur only at the beginning of a period and then taper off. Most girls find them noticeable but not bad enough to ruin their day. However, some girls have cramps that are more painful. Fortunately, there are many ways to deal with cramps to make them less unpleasant. (We'll talk more about handling cramps and other period bummers in Chapter 6.)

One thing's for sure—the more you learn about what to expect with your own period, the easier it will be to handle any problems that come up. And learning these things just takes a little time and patience.

∾4∾

WHAT TO WEAR

You've probably seen ads for some of the things girls wear to absorb their period flow. But until you actually go to buy something for yourself, you may not realize how many choices there are! One look at a drugstore shelf crammed with different brands of maxi pads, superabsorbent tampons, panty liners, overnight pads, pads with wings, long pads, regular tampons, light-day pads, tampons with applicators, tampons without applicators, even cups—and you may feel like giving up.

Don't worry! Figuring out what to wear isn't as hard as it seems. In spite of all that variety, the choices pretty much boil down to two—either some type of pad or some type of tampon.

Let's start with pads. They're the easiest to use, so most girls start out with them when they first get their periods. Pads are worn inside your underpants, attached to the crotch. They are made of soft cotton and have a plastic lining on the bottom to keep blood from soaking through and staining your clothes. Some also have plastic "wings" on the sides for extra protection. On the bottom is a sticky strip that keeps the pad attached to your underpants. Pads come in different thicknesses for heavier or lighter periods and in different widths and lengths to fit different body shapes. Panty liners are like pads, only much thinner and less absorbent. They are basically intended to soak up your vaginal discharge and keep it from staining your underpants. But some girls with very light flows use panty liners as pads, while other girls wear them as protection in case they get their periods unexpectedly.

Tampons are also made of cotton, but they are shaped like a lipstick tube so they can fit inside your vagina. Some kinds of tampons come with a throwaway cardboard or plastic applicator to help you put the tampon inside you. Others are just inserted with your finger. All tampons have a string at one end so you can pull the tampon out when it's time to remove it. Tampons also come in different sizes to fit your shape and different absorbencies to fit the amount of your period flow. (While we're talking about things that fit inside your vagina, there are also cups that catch the blood. But since they are trickier to insert, they're more for older girls.)

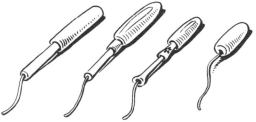

As you can see, there are some big differences between pads and tampons. But they have a lot in common too. Both are easy to use. Both are comfortable. Both come in different sizes to fit your shape and different absorbencies to fit the amount of your period flow. And best of all, no one can tell if you're wearing either one of them.

WHICH IS BETTER?

The answer to that is entirely up to you. If you're like most girls, you'll probably find you like one better than the other. But both have some special advantages.

For example, one reason that many girls like pads is that they're so easy to use. Even a beginner can put one on with no trouble. Just take off the piece of paper covering the sticky strip and place the pad in the middle of the crotch of your underpants, the sticky strip down. Then press down a little so the pad sticks tightly to your underpants, and you're ready to go!

On the other hand, pads take up more space in your bag than a tampon. If you're going somewhere very dressy and are carrying a tiny purse, it can be hard to find enough room to fit in a pad.

"I'm going to wear pads for sure. Tampons kind of freak me out! I don't want something inside me. That's creepy!"

The biggest disadvantage of a pad is that you can't really go swimming with one on. As you can imagine, as soon as it gets wet, you have a squishy, soaked, uncomfortable glob of cotton between your legs. Even if you decide not to go in the water, a pad may be too bulky to wear with a bathing suit.

Being able to go swimming is one of the reasons many girls like tampons. Because they fit inside of you where water doesn't go, they don't get soggy like pads do. Also, since only the string is outside of your body, a tampon is completely invisible, so you can wear it with any kind of bathing suit. Dancers and girls who play active sports usually like tampons better too. And because they are worn inside the body, many girls feel cleaner wearing a tampon instead of a pad.

"I told my mom that I want to use tampons when I get my period. She thought I was too young, but she asked the doctor and he said it was okay even for girls my age. So she said I could."

Tampons are also easier to carry around. In fact, some are so small, they can fit in the back pocket of tight jeans without even being noticeable. And you can usually put a couple into even a tiny purse. Finally, when they're in correctly, you can't even feel them at all. Many girls like the fact that tampons let them feel more like their everyday, nonperiod selves.

A LITTLE SCARY ...

But there are some drawbacks to tampons too. Probably the biggest one is that you have to learn how to insert them. Although putting in a tampon is really very easy, some girls find the idea a little creepy, if not downright scary. They worry that they might hurt themselves putting a tampon in or that the tampon might get lost or "go up inside them." Other girls think that virgins (girls who haven't had sex yet) aren't supposed to use tampons, or that using them means you're not a virgin anymore.

Luckily, none of this is true. You won't hurt yourself by putting in a tampon. Remember, the walls of your vagina are elastic and can expand. So even though a tampon may look too big to fit inside of you at first, it's really much smaller than your vagina.

A tampon can't get lost inside of you because there's nowhere for it to go. Your cervix blocks the opening from your vagina to your uterus, so it can't go any farther up inside of you. It has to stay in your vagina until you decide to take it out.

Girls who are virgins usually have a hymen stretched across the opening of their vagina. That's why some people have the mistaken idea that these girls can't or shouldn't use tampons. They think the hymen has to be broken in order to put in a tampon. But when you think about it, that doesn't make sense. After all, your hymen already has a hole or several holes in it—that's how your period blood flows out of you in the first place. So it is perfectly all right for you to use tampons.

Since both pads and tampons have advantages, many girls use both. They may pick tampons for a day at the beach, but choose pads for the rest of the time. Other girls who generally prefer tampons may find wearing them uncomfortable on days when they have cramps and choose pads for those times.

PRACTICING

Do you ever wonder what it feels like to wear a pad? The best way to find out is to try one and see. In fact, it's a good idea to do this before you actually need a pad. That way, you'll know what to expect when the time comes. If you're like most girls, you'll probably prefer a thinner pad to start with.

It's also a good idea to practice wearing a tampon at least once, even if you're pretty sure you prefer pads. That's because in an emergency, a tampon may be all that's available. It's a lot less nerve-racking to learn how to put in a tampon in your own home than when you're stuck in a strange bathroom, trying to read a tiny instruction sheet. Also, sooner or later, you'll probably find you have your period just on the day you'd planned to go to the beach. By practicing, you'll already know what to do.

PUTTING IN A TAMPON

Whether you're just practicing or using one for real, here are some no-hassle hints for putting in a tampon. First, be sure to buy a slim or thin size, not a regular or super size. The slender tampons are smaller and easier to learn with.

Remember, tampons come with a cardboard or plastic applicator or are inserted with your finger. If using just your finger seems gross, try one with an applicator. Better yet, try them both and see which you like best.

The secret to putting in a tampon is to relax. If you're a little uptight about sticking something up your vagina, that's natural. You haven't had any experience with this before, so it may seem a little weird at first.

Usually, people put in tampons while they are sitting on the toilet. You can do this if you want. But for the first time, it may be easier to relax if you lie on your back on your bed.

To start with, let's talk about the ones with an applicator. You may want to experiment with one of these outside your body before actually trying to insert it, so that you can see how it works. Either way, the first step is to remove the paper wrapping and check to make sure that the string is hanging out the bottom. The applicator has a small tube inside of a bigger tube. Use your thumb and middle finger to hold on to the bottom of the big tube. Then slide the front end of the tube into your vagina. Aim toward your lower back, and push the tube in far enough so that your fingers touch your body.

Now push the smaller tube into the larger tube. You can use your index finger for this or a finger on your other hand. As the smaller tube slides in, it pushes the tampon into your vagina. The applicator places the tampon behind your pubic bone (the bony ridge around the opening of your vagina), so you shouldn't have to give it an extra nudge to get it in any farther. Just pull out the applicator, and you're done! Although some applicators can be flushed down the toilet, most can't. You'll probably need to wrap the applicator in toilet paper and toss it in a trash can.

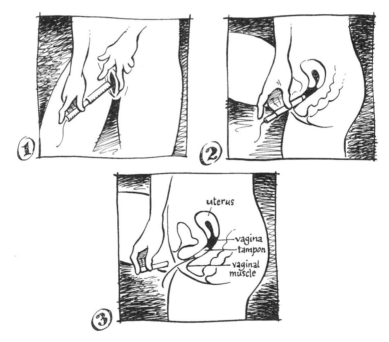

What about tampons that don't have applicators? Putting in one of these isn't much different from putting in an applicator tampon. The only difference is that you use your finger to push the tampon inside of you instead of the small applicator tube. Although it's important to wash your hands before inserting any kind of tampon, this is especially true when using the kind that you insert with your finger.

Take off the wrapping and make sure the string is hanging out of the bottom. Hold the tampon between your thumb and index or middle finger, and push it into your vagina. When it is in as far as it will go this way, nudge it in a little farther by pushing on the bottom of the tampon with one finger. Make sure you get it past your pubic bone. When the tampon is in correctly, you shouldn't be able to feel that it's there at all. If you can feel it, you probably haven't pushed it past the bone.

Now that the tampon is in, how do you get it out? Simple! That's what the string is for. Gently pull on the string and pull the tampon out.

For some of you, putting in a tampon may be so easy that you wonder what the big deal is. But many girls get a little nervous the first time they try. If that happens to you, just slow down, take a deep breath, and wait a minute or two. Since tampons are harder to put in when you're nervous, relaxing will make everything go much easier. You should have better luck the second time around.

TIME FOR A CHANGE

After a while, both pads and tampons have soaked up all the blood that they can hold and need to be changed. Pads should be changed every three or four hours, even on days when your flow is light and the pad may take longer than that to get used up. Changing them frequently—even before they are completely full—keeps pads from developing a slight odor.

On days when your period is heaviest, your pads may fill up more quickly and need to be changed more often. Fortunately, since pads are worn outside your body, you can tell just by looking at them if they are getting filled sooner than you expected.

When you are finished with a pad or a tampon, wrap it up in toilet paper and drop it in a trash can. In many public bathrooms, there are special little cans in each stall. Be careful not to flush pads or tampons down the toilet, as they can clog it up. That's not only embarrassing for you, but gross for the next person who has to use the toilet!

Tampons should also be changed every three or four hours. Like pads, they may have to be changed more frequently on days when your period is heaviest. But since tampons are inside your body, you can't just take a look to make sure they aren't being used up faster than you expected. This means that you have to be careful to remember when you put the last one in.

If you're worried your tampon may soak through unexpectedly, you can always wear a panty liner to be safe.

There's another reason for being sure to remember when you put the tampon in. Because you can't feel a tampon once it's in, it's easy to forget you are wearing one. This is especially true on your last day, when you are hardly bleeding. Since little to no blood soaks through, there's nothing to remind you.

TOXIC SHOCK SYNDROME

It can be tempting to leave the same tampon in all day when your flow is very light. This is *not* a good idea, however! Leaving a tampon in for a long time increases the chance of getting a disease called toxic shock syndrome. Toxic shock syndrome is *very, very* rare, but it is also very serious. Although anyone can get this disease—including women who no longer get their periods, and men—it happens most often in women wearing tampons.

Tampons themselves don't cause toxic shock syndrome. It's caused by bacteria. But when tampons are left in too long, they can be a breeding ground for these germs. That's why changing your tampons regularly is so important.

Another thing you can do to avoid this disease is to use only the absorbency you really need. Some girls with a lighter flow think that if they use a superabsorbent tampon, they won't have to bother changing it for a whole day. As you can see, this is an especially bad idea!

KEEPING "FRESH"

In the United States, people are extremely worried about smelling bad. You probably already know about all the deodorants, mouthwashes, breath mints, foot sprays, and other things that are supposed to make your body and breath smell better. It's hard to find people who don't use at least one of these products.

Bathing, wearing clean clothes, and brushing your teeth regularly can often be enough to keep stinky odors away. But if you want to use some of these products, that's okay. Even if you don't really need them, they may make you feel more confident. And unless you have an allergy to something in one of these items, they are unlikely to harm you.

But you may also have heard advertisements suggesting that women and girls have to be particularly worried about "staying fresh" at certain times of the month. While they don't come right out and say so, they imply that the area around your vagina smells bad or that you have a nasty odor when you are having your period.

Needless to say, this idea is really upsetting, especially if you've just started having your period. After all, the last thing you want is to have an obnoxious odor announcing to everyone that you're having your period!

You'll be glad to know that this is one thing you don't have to worry about. If you're healthy, bathe daily (including washing between your legs), wear clean underpants, and change your pads or tampons regularly when you're having your period, you don't need these special products. And you don't need to worry that your genitals may have a bad odor or that other people can tell by your smell that you're having your period. It just isn't true!

Embarrassing!

Sometimes, things happen around your period that can be really embarrassing. But when you think about them later, they're pretty funny. Here are some that have happened to other girls that they thought might make you laugh.

"Once, when I tossed my bag down, a tampon rolled out right in front of these boys in my class. I just about had a heart attack, but my friend grabbed it before they got a good look, and we just walked away."

*"Our dog, Rebel, likes to get into trash cans. One day the new minister from our church came to the house to introduce himself. My mom and I were sitting there talking to him when Rebel tore out of the bathroom with a **used bloody pad** in his mouth. My mom and I **freaked out** and chased him around the room, trying to get it, but Rebel thought we were playing. Finally, he ran under the coffee table and started shredding it. The minister pretended nothing unusual was happening, but we were really embarrassed."*

"Last year, when I was eleven, my mom took me hiking on a trail in the Chiricahua National Park. I was having my period but forgot to bring something to wrap my used tampon in, so she said just to dig a hole and bury it because it was biodegradable and wouldn't hurt the environment. But the ground was really hard and I didn't have anything to dig with, so that didn't work. Then she said to throw it way off the path into the trees. I threw it as hard as I could, but the string got tangled in a tree branch over my head, so now the whole thing was hanging over the middle of the path where anyone who looked up just a little could see it. We tried to get it down, but it was too high to reach. Finally, my mom said, 'Let's just get out of here before someone comes along!' So we turned around and went back the way we came."

∼ 5 ∾

"IS THIS NORMAL?"

Do you sometimes worry about whether the changes happening (or not happening) to you are normal? If so, you're not alone! A *lot* of girls feel that way! Since they don't know exactly what to expect, it's easy to be afraid that something may go wrong. One way many girls try to find out if everything is going the way it's supposed to is by comparing themselves to other girls their age. They figure that if they are like everyone else, they must be okay.

The only problem with this is that "normal" and "like everyone else" are often not the same. When people say that a person's body is normal, they mean that it's healthy and developing the way it should. On the other hand, when they say "like everyone else," they don't really mean like *everyone* else, but like most of the people they know or want to be like.

Sometimes being like your friends can seem almost as important as being normal. But in reality there's a big difference! In a year or two, many of the things that make you feel different from your friends now, such as being the first girl in your class to get your period, no longer matter. Other differences that you disliked when you were younger, such as being the tallest girl in your school, may be one of the things you like best about yourself when you are older.

Of course, if something going on with you is really not normal, you need a doctor's help. Sometimes girls can be so worried that something is wrong with them that they are afraid to check it out with an adult to see if it's true. That means a lot of girls worry about things that are perfectly normal, while others may be hiding problems that actually need attention.

If you're worried that something about you isn't normal, don't be afraid to talk to your mom, another adult woman whom you're comfortable with, or a doctor about the problem. They can help you understand what's happening and whether or not everything's okay. And if there is a problem, they can help to fix it.

It may also help you to read about some of the things other girls worry about:

"My left breast is smaller than my right one! Everyone said that it would eventually catch up with the other breast, but it hasn't. What's wrong with me?"

It's very common for one breast to start developing before the other. Usually, the slower breast does catch up, but occasionally it doesn't. It's perfectly normal to have breasts that are slightly different in size, or to have one breast that is a little lower than the other, or to have one breast pointing straight ahead while the other points a little to the side.

Although these differences are normal, that doesn't mean you like them. If you're in this situation, you may be afraid that other kids have noticed that your breasts aren't identical and think you look funny. It's good to keep in mind that people really can't tell whether your breasts are the same or different, especially when you have clothes on. However, if you're really bothered by this or if you have breasts that are very different in size, there are bra inserts you can use that will even out the way your breasts look.

"Lately, I have this wet stuff that comes out of my vagina. It's not my period, because it isn't bloody. There's so much of it that it soaks through my underpants. I can't even wear tights anymore because I'm worried it looks like I peed in my pants. What is it? Is there a pill I can take to make it stop?"

If you remember from Chapter 2, this wet stuff is your body's way of flushing out your vagina and keeping it clean and stretchy, so you don't want to make it stop. It's also the reason why you may have begun to see yellowish stains on your underpants. As long as this discharge is a clear milky white or yellowish color, it's perfectly normal. What is *not* normal is a discharge that is brownish or greenish, looks like cottage cheese, has a sickly sweet or really bad smell, or makes you itch. These things are signs that you have an infection and need to see a doctor.

Usually, this discharge isn't enough to soak through underpants and tights, but some girls have a heavier discharge than average. Although this amount is normal for you, no one likes feeling wet, uncomfortable, and self-conscious. This is when panty liners really come in handy! Fortunately, panty liners are skinny and can easily fit in a bag or even a back pocket, so you can take extra ones wherever you go. Just be sure to change them frequently. You'll be more comfortable and your clothes will stay dry.

"I'm really worried! My period isn't just blood. There are blobs of red, jellylike stuff too. Are parts of my insides falling out?"

These blobs are a normal part of your period, but if you aren't prepared for them, they can be a little disturbing. When you have your period, your uterus is shedding dead cells as well as blood, and they mix with secretions that are being discharged too. Together, they make up the blobs you're talking about. You're most likely to see these blobs on days when your period is heaviest.

"I had my first period four months ago, and my second period came the next month. But since then, I haven't had a period. I'm afraid to say anything to my mom, because I've heard that when a girl doesn't have her period, it means she's pregnant. But, honestly—I've never had sex! Could I be pregnant anyway?"

Being pregnant is only one of many reasons why a girl may not get her period for a couple of months.

Girls are often very irregular when they first start having their periods. They may have two periods in a month and a half, and not have another one for several months. It can take a couple of years for their bodies to settle down to a regular routine. And even then, they're not likely to have their periods at *exactly* the same time each month.

Even grown women who are very regular often find that things like stress, emotional upsets, sickness, or traveling make their periods come earlier or later than usual. Finally, the regular routine for some girls is to be irregular, with very different amounts of time between their periods. It may be harder for them to know when to expect their periods, but this pattern is normal for them.

So you shouldn't worry about talking to your mom about what's going on with your periods. In fact, she may have had the same thing happen to her when she was your age and would like the chance to share her experiences with you.

*"I've started having this **awful** itching around my vagina, and it hurts when I pee! I have to try really hard not to reach down and scratch myself in class. Why is this happening and how do I get rid of it?"*

Although only a doctor can tell for sure, it sounds like you have a yeast infection. And yeast infections can make you feel miserable! Ordinarily, your immune system keeps the small amount of yeast that's normally in your vagina in check. But some things, such as lack of sleep, being stressed out, being sick, and taking certain medicines, such as antibiotics, can make it more likely that the yeast will get out of control.

Fortunately, yeast infections can be easily treated. But you should check with your doctor first so he or she can decide which medicine is best for you.

There are also some things you can do to prevent getting another yeast infection. Since yeast grows best in moist places, change out of wet swimsuits and sweaty exercise clothes as soon as possible. If you find you're getting really sweaty in gym, you may even want to keep a change of underwear (or a new panty liner) for after class. Wear cotton underpants, because they absorb moisture better than underwear made of synthetic material. Change tampons and pads often during your period. It's also a good idea to change panty liners frequently, especially if you have heavy vaginal discharge. Finally, it's best to avoid scented products like bubble baths and sprays, as well as pads and tampons that have scents added.

*"I bleed a lot when I get my period. And I mean **a lot**! My period just doesn't seem to stop. No one I know has periods like these."*

The amount of blood in a period may look like a lot, but it's usually not as much as it seems. Most girls lose anywhere from a couple of spoonfuls to a cup of blood with each period. Since it doesn't take a lot of blood to use up a tampon or pad, it can be hard to judge exactly how much you are bleeding. But if you find that you are completely drenching entire pads or tampons one right after another so that you have to change them every hour for a whole day, you are probably bleeding too much and should see a doctor.

The length of a period and the time between periods can also vary, even a lot, and still be normal. Some girls bleed for only a couple of days, while others have periods that last seven or eight days. But if your period is this long, it should definitely be tapering off by the seventh day. And it should stop completely a day or two after that.

If your periods really aren't stopping or are coming with only a few days in between, it's important that you see a doctor. Just as you may be finding all the changes around your period confusing, your body may be having trouble getting things together too. Your doctor can make sure you don't lose too much blood, and can get your period on track.

"I thought pubic hair was just supposed to be down by your legs, but mine is growing in a line halfway up to my belly button. Plus, I'm getting a mustache! I look like a man!"

In some girls, it's natural for pubic hair to grow onto their upper thighs or up toward their belly button. They may even begin to get darker hair on their upper lip. There is nothing wrong with this, and it certainly doesn't mean that these girls are somehow less feminine.

In our culture, however, having less hair in these places is often seen as more attractive. So, while it's normal to have hair that grows a little farther up your abdomen or on your lip, you may not be too happy about it.

If you are one of these girls, there are a couple of ways you can handle this situation. One is to decide whether it's really as bad as you think. For example, the hairs on your lip that look like a man's mustache to you may be hardly noticeable to other people.

There are ways of removing or bleaching this hair. But there are some things you definitely should *not* do. One of them is trying to shave the hair off your upper lip. This will leave you with icky stubble and will probably make the hair grow back darker and thicker. Also, some chemical hair removers can burn or scar your skin. So avoid using them on your face unless you have your parents' permission.

If you are unhappy about hair on your face or pubic area, why not talk it over with your mom? She may have had the same problem and discovered some good solutions.

"I'm getting these yucky white lines on my breasts. It looks like my skin is starting to tear apart. What's happening?"

These are stretch marks. They can show up anyplace on your body where the skin has grown very rapidly and lost some of its elasticity. Although you may not like the way they look, it doesn't mean your skin is going to rip

apart. And you'll be glad to know that they usually fade and become less noticeable with time.

> *"I'm in the fifth grade. Everyone I know is dying to get their periods, but **I don't want it!** Why can't I just stay the way I am?"*

Although they may not admit it, lots of girls don't want to start having periods. If you're a very young girl, getting your period way before any of your friends may seem really unfair. All of a sudden, you have to worry about cramps, counting the days between periods, carrying pads or tampons to school, and not bleeding through your clothes when no one else you know has to bother with these things. And if you're only nine, ten, or eleven years old, the idea that you are on the way to becoming a woman can be really upsetting and scary, especially if you don't think you've had enough time to be a kid.

Even if you're a little older, you may not be too happy about the fact that your body is maturing. All the talk about how you are "becoming a young woman" may seem to mean that you

have to start acting like an adult and can no longer do some of the fun kid things that you love doing. Or that you are suddenly supposed to become interested in other things—like makeup and boys—when you could care less.

There's nothing you can do to slow down or hurry up the changes that are happening in your body. *But you don't have to change your feelings or your interests until you're ready!* Getting your period does not mean you have to become someone different. You're still you! Remember, there are all different types of women and all kinds of ways to be a woman. Right now you're still a kid, so enjoy your childhood. You have plenty of time to figure out what kind of woman you want to be.

∽ 6 ∾

PUBERTY BUMMERS AND HOW TO HANDLE THEM

Very few girls experience all the puberty bummers talked about here, at least not all the time. But you'll probably have one or two of these problems at some point or another. These problems tend to go away or lessen after a few years as your body gets used to the changes it's going through. So just because you may be bothered with some of these bummers now doesn't mean you'll be stuck with them for the rest of your life. And, with a little practice, you'll learn how to handle the ones that you do have so that they don't mess up your life.

PIMPLES OR "ZITS"

Chances are, if you're going through puberty, you've seen signs of pimples or "zits" on your face. Of course, boys are just as likely to get pimples as girls. But many girls have a tendency to break out when they're having their periods, so they're often more concerned about zits then.

Pimples are caused when a pore in your skin becomes clogged with oil and infected. That means that the most important thing you can do to prevent them is to keep your skin clean. That way, there is less chance that oil will build up on your skin and, if it does, less chance that there is bacteria around to cause infection.

Keeping your skin clean means washing your face in the morning and before you go to bed. It does *not* mean scrubbing your face until it's raw or washing it a zillion times a day. You don't want your skin to get so dry that it has to produce extra oil to compensate. That will only make things worse.

Keeping your face clean also means keeping your hair clean. Greasy or dirty hair that touches your face adds extra oil and bacteria to your skin. Some girls whose foreheads have a tendency to break out wear bangs to hide the problem, not realizing that oily bangs may be causing the pimples in the first place. Since pimples can also break out on your shoulders and back, you should keep these areas clean too.

By the way, one thing that you don't have to worry about is avoiding foods like pizza, fried food, and chocolate. While there are other reasons not to eat too much of these things, they don't cause pimples, so you can eat them without increasing your risk of a zit attack.

Every single book that talks about pimples tells you not to pick at them or pop them because this may leave permanent scars. And every single one of these books is right! But many girls go ahead and pop their pimples anyway. Although this is a bad practice, if you're determined to do it, at least wash your hands and face (or wherever the pimple is) first.

As you know from ads, there are lots of soaps, lotions, and creams available to prevent pimples or help them go away. Some of them are designed especially for oily, dry, or combination skin, while others are for use by anyone. If you're bothered by breakouts, these products can really help, although you may have to try a few to find the ones that work best for you. You also need to be patient, since it may take a couple of weeks for them to work.

Although most girls have only mild or occasional pimples, some have more serious skin problems, or acne. If you are one of these girls, you may want to ask your parents to take you to a special skin doctor called a dermatologist. A dermatologist can prescribe stronger

medications to help you deal with the situation, but be sure to take only ones that your doctor recommends.

If your parents tell you that your acne will "go away in a few years" or that you should "quit making a big deal out of a few zits," and that seeing a doctor isn't necessary, try letting them know how acne makes you feel and the effect it has on your self-confidence. If it's serious enough to make you feel bad about yourself, it's serious enough to get help for the problem.

The good news about pimples is that you usually won't have to live with them forever. They tend to occur most often when you are going through puberty. Although adults can be bothered by acne as well, by the time you reach your twenties, pimples may be pretty much a thing of the past.

SWOLLEN OR TENDER BREASTS

Some girls find that their breasts become swollen or tender around the time of their periods. Usually, this is only

slightly uncomfortable, but sometimes it can be painful or irritating. If you are bothered by tenderness and have small breasts that don't need much support, you may want to go without a bra on these days. On the other hand, if you have larger breasts or will be playing a sport that makes your breasts jiggle around, wearing a bra with extra support may help you feel more comfortable.

CRAMPS

Ugh, cramps! As mentioned in Chapter 3, cramps are a pain or ache in your abdomen that can occur during your period. Some girls rarely have cramps, others have them more often, and a few get them every month. Since cramps can vary from mild to severe, what you do about them depends on how bad you are feeling.

If your cramps are mild and last a day or less, you can probably just ignore them. But if they make you too uncomfortable to do that, then there are plenty of other things you can do to make yourself feel

better. Heat helps to relieve cramps, so you can try taking a long, hot bath or placing a heating pad or hot-water bottle on your stomach. Gently rubbing or massaging your abdomen can help to relax cramping muscles and make the cramps less painful. Many girls find that gentle stretching exercises, taking a walk, or riding a bike may also help you to feel better, particularly if you have mild cramps. But you will probably want to pick activities that aren't super-energetic on days when you have cramps. For example, this can be a good time to read a book or watch a movie you've been wanting to see.

Non-aspirin pain pills or medications designed especially for period cramps are sold at any drugstore, and these may be enough to make you feel okay and able to do the things you normally do. However, do not take any of these pain pills without your parents' permission. Some, like aspirin, are okay for adults but may be harmful to children or teenagers under certain circumstances. As is the case with all pain medications, it's important to take the lowest effective dose, because too much may be harmful. What if nothing seems to work and you have painful cramps that make you miserable almost every month? If this is the case, your cramps are a world-class bummer! Only people who have never had them would be silly enough to say that you're making a big deal out of nothing! If you have monster cramps frequently, you need to go to a gynecologist—a doctor who specializes in women's reproductive systems—to get help. Your gynecologist can figure out why you are having such severe cramps and can come up with a solution that will make you feel better.

MOOD SWINGS

Along with puberty, many girls find themselves having weird mood swings. Sometimes they get really annoyed at things that don't normally bother them. At other times their feelings are more easily hurt than is usually the case. Then, the next day, everything seems fine again. Mood swings can happen anytime, so they aren't just period bummers. But they are even more common when you are having your period.

It may surprise you to know that some girls actually feel in a better mood when they are having their periods. But since they don't complain about feeling good, you're not likely  to hear much about this. What you are likely to hear about are the emotions girls wish they weren't having, such as feeling sad or cranky.

Of course, if you're in the middle of having painful

cramps, you're probably not going to be
in a great mood. But sometimes you
may feel a little depressed, irritable, or
touchy around the time of your period,
even if there doesn't seem to be any
reason for you to be feeling this way.

GRRRRR

There isn't a whole lot you can do to
change the way you feel at these times. But
there are things you can do to handle these
feelings. First, don't try to feel something that you're
not. There's no law that says you have to go around
pretending to be happy when you really feel a little sad.
Instead of hanging out with your friends as usual, do
you just want to be alone? Then go home and listen to
music or take a walk or do whatever you feel is right for
you. You may want to explain to your friends why you
don't feel like being with them, but that's up to you.

Second, if you know that you get really sensitive
around the time of your period, try to remember that.
If something upsets you, ask yourself if it's really as
bad as it seems or whether your reaction might be
partly due to the fact that you're having your period.

As you get used to all the changes you're going through,
you'll have a better idea of what puberty bummers to
expect. You'll also discover your own best ways of

handling them. But other girls can suggest some ideas you may not have thought of. In fact, you may find that it's kind of fun to trade solutions with your friends or older sisters or your mother.

∽ 7 ↩

"WHAT IF . . . ?"

W┃hen you first start having your period, it can seem as if you suddenly have to be on guard for all sorts of things that could be awkward or embarrassing. Some of the things you may worry about could very well happen, while others aren't very likely. Either way, it helps to know ahead of time how to handle some of these situations, such as . . .

"What if I get my period at school?"

Except for getting your period at home, school is actually one of the better places for this to happen. That's because every nurse's office has a supply of pads on hand for just this emergency.

How you handle getting your period at school

depends on several things. If you discover your period when you go to the bathroom, you have a couple of choices. If there's only a small stain on your underpants, you can get a pad or tampon from the bathroom dispenser or the nurse's office and go back to class. If, by chance, you've bled a lot and your mom is home, you may want to give her a call and ask her to bring you some clean clothes. In any case, the school nurse will give you a pass that excuses you for being late getting back to class.

On occasion, you may be in class when you discover you've gotten your period. It may be that your underpants have suddenly become very wet or you actually feel blood dripping out. If this happens, raise your hand and ask to be excused. Then go to the bathroom and check things out.

*"What if I bleed through to the back of my skirt or pants, **and people can see it?**"*

This happens to almost everyone at some time in her life (or at least almost everyone is afraid it will), so it's good to know that there are plenty of things you can do.

If you are wearing
a sweater, sweatshirt,
or long-sleeved shirt
that you can take off,
just tie it casually
around your waist so
that it covers the spot.
Then go to a bathroom
and get a tampon or pad.
If you don't have anything
to tie over the spot and you're

wearing a skirt, sometimes you can just turn the skirt
around so the spot is in the front, and hold your bag or
books in front of it until you can get to a bathroom. You
can also ask a friend to lend you something. Probably
the most common solution is just to have another girl
to walk behind you to the bathroom. That way no one
(except her, of course) can see what happened.

It's a good idea to keep a spare skirt or pair of
pants in your backpack or schoolbag. Even if you
never need them, you'll feel safer knowing they are
there in case of an emergency. You may also want
to wear a panty liner on the days right before you
expect your period, since surprises can happen.
Finally, try to wear darker-colored skirts or pants
when you have your period, at least on days when

your flow is heaviest. Often, bloodstains aren't even visible on dark material.

> *"What if I get my period when I don't expect it and there isn't any way to buy a pad or a tampon?"*

If the flow at the beginning of your period is usually light, you probably won't have to do anything at all. Your underpants will get a little stained, but you can always wash them out later. Unless you're going to be away from home (or a drugstore) for a really long time, blood probably won't soak through to your outer clothing.

On the other hand, if there's a chance that you will bleed through your underpants to your skirt or your pants, you'll want to do something to keep that from happening. If there's a public bathroom around, you're in luck. Just fold a thick layer of toilet paper or paper towels, and place it in the crotch of your underpants like you do with a pad. If you're worried the toilet paper may fall out, wrap it around the crotch to keep it in place. This will probably hold you over until you get home or to someplace where you can buy a pad or a tampon.

Although it isn't very likely, it's possible you will get your period unexpectedly in a place where there isn't any toilet paper—like on a long hike in the woods, for example. Or maybe your flow is very heavy at the beginning of your period, and toilet paper just won't be enough. In these situations, you probably have something in your bag or on your body that would make a good emergency pad. Socks work pretty well, by the way. So do bandannas and headbands. Remember, you can always wash them out afterward.

A Sock!

Most important, don't forget that other girls and women can be a big help if you're stranded without a pad or a tampon. Since they've all been in this predicament at some time (or have at least worried that they will be), they can all imagine what you feel. Many people carry an emergency pad or tampon with them, and even total strangers will be perfectly happy to give you one if they don't need it.

> *"My parents are divorced, and I spend every other weekend with my dad. What if I get my first period when I'm at his house?"*

This is a good situation to plan for, since it could very well happen. If you have a dresser drawer of your own in your dad's house, a smart thing to do is to store a box of pads or tampons there, just in case. Even if your first period doesn't come while you're at his place, chances are that a future period will, and you'll be glad you're prepared.

But what if you are on vacation with your dad? Or you don't have a place of your own to put things in his house? Or you get your period before you've had a chance to store some pads? Don't panic! If you have a stepmother or stepsister and you're close enough to talk to them about this, they'll be glad to help.

Even if your dad lives alone or you don't want to discuss this with members of your stepfamily, you still have someone you can turn to—him! It may surprise you, but fathers know a lot about periods. Any man who has lived with a woman for any length of time knows what periods are, what pads and tampons are for, and what women experience when they have their periods. They also know it's a very natural part of a woman's life.

In fact, even if you don't need your dad's help, you might still want to let him know that you've gotten your first period. Chances are he'll feel flattered and happy that you're including him in this important event—even if he acts flustered or nervous. And if he does seem a little uncomfortable, it's only because he hasn't had much practice dealing with you on this level and is worried he won't respond the way you want him to.

"What if I can't get a tampon out?"

A lot of girls worry about this, even when they know a tampon can't get "lost" inside of them. In this case, you can relax! *Getting a tampon out is almost never a problem.* The most common fear— that the string may break off—just doesn't seem to happen. The only time you may run into difficulty is when  the string has somehow been pushed into your vagina so that you can't get ahold of it. And the only time this is likely to happen is if you tucked it into your vagina so that it wouldn't hang out of a bathing suit.

In the rare case that a string does get pushed inside of you, you'll have to go in after it. While this may seem a bit creepy, it really isn't hard.

The first step is to take a deep breath and relax. Then put your index or your middle finger (because it's longer) into your vagina and feel around for the string. It's usually easy to find. Now comes the tricky part.

Because it's been in your vagina, the string is probably pretty slippery, which makes it harder to grab. If you can, scoop it toward the opening of your vagina so that you can use both your finger and your thumb to pull it out. If that doesn't work, try to wrap the string around your finger so that when you pull it out, it won't slip off.

If you can't find the string or are having a problem grabbing it, just go for the tampon itself. Hook your finger behind it and pull it down toward the opening of your vagina. Or you can often get ahold of the tampon by squeezing it between your index and middle fingers. Sometimes, pushing down as if you were going to the bathroom will help to move it toward the entrance of your vagina.

Don't get frustrated if you don't get the tampon out on the first try. Remember, it's not going anywhere, so you'll get it out eventually.

"What if I go to buy pads or tampons and the checkout clerk is a boy I know?"

It can be embarrassing to buy period products or medications for a yeast infection from someone you know, or even from a male you don't know. There are several ways you can handle this situation. Of course, if you have a choice of stores, you can shop in one where this isn't a problem, even if it means going out of your way. But if you live in a small town, this may be the only place available. Until you're more comfortable with things, you can ask your mother or older sister if she will pick up pads or tampons for you.

But a better way to deal with this may be to decide that you're not going to let it embarrass you. After all, most of the teenage girls and adult women in your town use these products, so chances are that this particular boy has probably already sold them to several people whom he knows. If he's cool at all, he should know that having periods is a normal part of being female. If he's a jerk, who cares what he thinks?

"What if my mother hasn't said anything to me yet about getting my period? How do I get her to talk to me?"

There may be several reasons why your mom hasn't brought up this subject. If you are only nine or ten, she may not be aware that girls your age can get their periods, especially if she was fourteen or fifteen when she first started. So she may mistakenly be waiting to talk to you about getting your period until you've reached the age when she thinks it's possible that this could happen to you.

MORE COOKIES, DEAR?

If you're older, your mom may be hesitating because she isn't exactly sure how to approach the subject. Maybe *her* mother never really talked to her or was so embarrassed when she did that it made both of them uncomfortable. Because she cares about you and realizes this is important, she's probably very concerned about doing it right. But as you may know, often the more you worry about making mistakes, the harder it can be to do anything at all.

Whatever the reason your mom hasn't mentioned getting your period, if you'd like to be able to talk with her but don't know how to start, you can hand her this book and ask her if she agrees with what's written in it. Letting her know that you want to hear about her experiences can also get the ball rolling.

∽ 8 ∾

BRACES—THE NON-BUMMER

You've probably already seen some kids with braces on their teeth, so you know what braces are, but you may have wondered why anyone would get them. Since crooked teeth, teeth that stick out, or teeth that just look kind of goofy aren't considered as attractive as straight, even teeth, most people get braces to straighten their teeth and improve their appearance. But there are some good health reasons for getting braces as well. Over time,

teeth that don't fit together correctly can result in tooth decay, gum disease, and headaches and earaches, as well as problems speaking, biting, or chewing. And who needs that?

Since most people who need braces get them between the ages

97

of nine and fourteen—when they've lost most of their baby teeth, and most of their permanent teeth have grown in—braces are part of puberty for a lot of girls. But braces aren't part of puberty in the same way that the growth spurt is. In fact, more and more adults are getting braces in their thirties and forties, and they went through puberty ages ago!

Braces don't really qualify as a bummer either. Although some kids may dread having to wear braces, many girls (and boys) actually look forward to getting them! They don't like their crooked teeth and can hardly wait to get them straightened. And, since some of their friends are likely to have braces too, it's no big deal.

Braces have changed a lot from the ones your parents may have worn when they were teenagers. While the metal braces that fit around each tooth are still used, there are now white or clear braces that are a lot less noticeable. Some braces even fit behind the teeth, where they can't be seen. Other things are still the same. Many kids wear headgear attached to their braces while they sleep to help reposition their teeth, and most will wear a retainer for a while, either in place of braces or after they get their braces off.

How do you know if you need braces? Dentists say that by the time you are seven, your parents should take you to an orthodontist, a dentist who specializes in

braces, to see how your teeth and mouth are developing and to begin planning if it looks like braces would be a good idea for you.

If it turns out that you will need braces, the next decision is when to start. That depends on several things. There are lots of reasons why you may need braces, and when to get them depends on what type of problem you have. An underbite is when your lower jaw is too big or your upper jaw is too small. If this is your problem, the orthodontist will want to start between ages seven and nine, when your mouth is still growing. On the other hand, if you have an overbite, or buck teeth, you can wait a few years. Most kids get braces because their teeth are crooked. If you are one of these people, you may be able to start at eight or nine years old.

Although there are new kinds of braces available now, you don't necessarily get to choose the kind that you want. That depends a lot on your particular problem. But regardless of the kind you get or when you get them, you'll have to be extra-careful to take good care of your teeth while you're wearing braces.

Braces provide more places where food can get trapped, causing cavities. Your braces also make it easier for chewing gum or sticky foods such as caramel candy and fruit bars to get stuck in hard-to-reach places. Even the sugar in soft drinks can find more places to hide when you have braces, so it's best to avoid supersweet or super sticky foods and drinks altogether if you can. And, of course, you'll have to be sure to brush and floss after you eat. After all, you're wearing braces so your teeth will look better, not so they become full of holes!

You should also avoid eating hard foods like nuts and hard cookies, or even chewing ice, because this can damage your braces. If you do break part of your braces, tell your orthodontist right away. Broken braces can't do a thing to straighten your teeth!

How long does all this last? That depends on when you first get braces and how complicated your problem is. If you start when you are eight or nine, you may be out of braces by the time you are in middle school. But some kids who start early may have to go through a second round after a break with no braces. Kids who get braces when they are thirteen or fourteen will be in high school when their braces come off. Generally, you can count on having braces for one to three years, depending on the problem that needs to be fixed. After your braces come off, you will probably need to wear a retainer full-time for the first six months or so, and then only while you are sleeping for the next couple of years.

∽ 9 ∾

NO BODY IS PERFECT

Just because your body is developing the way it should, doesn't mean that you are happy with it. In fact, if you're like most girls, you probably aren't totally thrilled with your looks. Right now different parts of your body are growing at different rates, so it may seem like you are too small in some places and too big in others. And it doesn't help that your body probably doesn't look much like the perfect ones that you see in magazines, the movies, or on TV.

But before you start feeling bad because you don't look like a fashion model or a movie star, there's something you should know. Most of these women don't really look like that either—at least, not without a lot of help! Makeup artists cover pimples, hair stylists add extensions to make hair longer and fuller, and fashion designers create clothes that hide figure flaws.

Afterward, these women's photographs may be touched up to make their waists look smaller or their breasts rounder. With that kind of attention, you would look perfect too!

TOO THIN

With all the pressure in our culture to be thin, it may seem like the skinnier you are, the better. So it's understandable if you mistakenly think that you would be a lot happier if only you were thinner. If you hope to be a professional gymnast, dancer, model, or ice-skater, you may have been told that you would have a greater chance of success if you lost weight, even if this isn't the best advice for you in the long run. As a result, you may decide to diet even if you aren't overweight.

For some girls, however, trying to lose weight can be a disaster. You may have heard of two eating disorders, anorexia and bulimia, that result from an obsession with being thin. Both of these conditions can cause serious health problems. And, sadly, neither one ever makes a girl more attractive.

ANOREXIA

People with anorexia take dieting to an extreme, refusing to eat *anything* they think might be fattening. Many people with anorexia live almost completely on low-calorie vegetables like lettuce and carrots. They may also develop strange eating habits, like cutting their food into tiny pieces or refusing to eat in front of other people. Some use laxatives to help their body get rid of the little they do eat, or they exercise for long hours to burn up calories.

As you would expect, they do lose weight. A lot of it! So much that they look terrible. They appear to be starving because, in many cases, they are. Without a layer of fat over their bones, they look like walking skeletons. Their hair and nails become brittle, their skin becomes dry and yellowish, their bones lose calcium and are more likely to break, and their periods stop. Even more important, a starvation diet like this can damage their hearts and brains, sometimes fatally.

By now you're probably wondering why any girl would make herself look so awful on purpose. Perhaps the scariest thing about anorexia is that people with this condition lose the ability to tell what they really look like. Although they are literally skin and bones,

anorexics see a fat person when they look at themselves in the mirror.

Despite the fact that they are wasting away, people
with anorexia think they still need to keep their weight
down. Since getting better means they will have to gain
weight, they often don't want to accept help. However,
anorexia is a serious, life-threatening emotional disor-
der, and people with this condition need professional
counseling.

BULIMIA

Unlike anorexics, people with bulimia can look completely normal. Instead of starving themselves, bulimics
binge on food, stuffing themselves with huge amounts at
a time. After bingeing, they purge, getting rid of the food
they have just eaten by making themselves throw up or
by using enemas or laxatives.

Bulimics generally binge because they feel depressed,
stressed-out, or down on themselves, and eating makes
them feel better, at least for the moment. But unfortu-
nately, bingeing and purging can take over their lives,
turning into a vicious cycle that they can't stop. Being
out of control like this makes them feel ashamed and
even worse about themselves.

Since they usually binge and purge in secret, it can

be hard to know if someone is bulimic. But doctors and dentists can often tell because of the health problems bulimia causes. Stomach acid is strong stuff. Vomiting over and over bathes your teeth in stomach acid, which chews away at tooth enamel and leaves cavities in your teeth. Cavities and missing enamel on the backs of the teeth are some clues that let dentists know when a person is bulimic. Constantly throwing up can also cause sore throats, swollen salivary glands, stomach ulcers, heartburn, indigestion, and constipation. It can even throw off your body's electrical balance, causing an irregular heartbeat or even a heart attack. Misusing laxatives can lead to other serious problems with digestion and may even affect your ability to poop at all. Finally, like anorexia, bulimia may cause your periods to be irregular or stop. None of these are problems you want to have!

Like people with anorexia, girls with bulimia need professional help to overcome the problem and learn how to eat in a healthy way.

OVERWEIGHT

Although many girls needlessly worry that they are overweight, some are right to be concerned. More and more American children and teenagers are becoming obese, or seriously overweight. Obesity is more than being chubby or needing to lose a few pounds. Obese people are *unmistakably* fat. Being this overweight negatively affects both their self-esteem and their health, increasing the chances that they will develop diabetes or heart problems.

There are a number of reasons why more and more kids are becoming obese, but two of the most important are the large portion sizes that we have become used to eating and the fact that many kids get very little exercise.

WHAT ABOUT YOU?

It can be hard to know if you need to lose or gain weight or if you're just about where you should be. And if you do need to lose weight, you may not know how to go about doing it in the right way.

One way *not* to decide whether your weight is right for you is to compare yourself to women you see in magazines and the movies. Your body is still developing and hasn't completely gotten its act together yet. So it isn't fair to compare yourself to models and celebrities who are adults. In fact, many women who have great figures now looked a lot like you when they were your age.

It's also not a good idea to compare yourself to your friends. Because everyone is growing at different rates, how you and your friends look today may be very different from the way any of you will look in a year or two. Besides, bodies come in many different sizes and shapes. So what's right for a friend's body may not be right for yours.

Weighing yourself and looking up the results on a chart listing the "normal" weight for your height won't tell you for sure if you are the right weight either. Scales are great for letting you know if you are gaining or losing weight, but they're not as good at determining if you are the right weight for your body. One reason for this is that muscle weighs more than fat. That means that a girl who's very athletic may weigh more than a girl of the same height and clothing size who spends most of her time reading or watching TV.

In fact, the only way you can be sure if you are the right weight is to ask your doctor, who can determine if you are underweight, of normal weight, overweight, or obese. If you need to gain or lose weight, he or she will help you do this in the right way.

BEING AT YOUR BEST WEIGHT

Perhaps you weigh pretty much what you should, but you'd like to stay that way. Or maybe you do need to lose a pound or two. Obviously, starving yourself or bingeing and purging are definitely *not* the way to go. Whether you need to gain or lose weight or are the right weight already, one thing that your doctor will recommend is that you eat the things that your growing body needs. That means getting enough protein, vitamins, minerals, fiber, and other nutrients. The best way to do this is to eat a variety of meat, fish, dairy products, vegetables, fruits, and grains. Because calcium is so important when your bones are growing, you need to make especially sure that you choose some foods that provide this mineral.

Ten Easy Sources of Calcium

- Milk
- Cheese
- Plain yogurt
- Sunflower seeds
- Almonds
- Figs
- Spinach
- Kale
- Soybeans
- Tofu

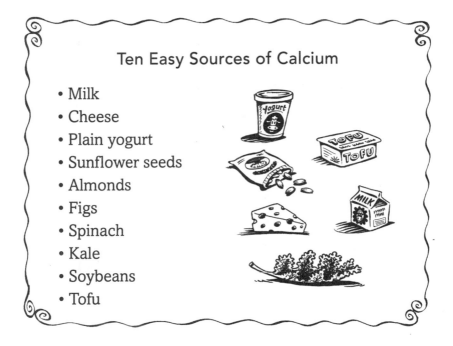

WHAT TO DO ABOUT SUGAR?

You may have noticed that some of your favorite things—like sodas, cookies, candy, doughnuts, and cake—are never mentioned in a list of healthy foods to eat. That's because all of them contain a lot of sugar and very little, if any, of the nutrients that your body needs. Other favorites, such as chips and French fries, are heavy in fat. Excess sugar and fat may taste good, but they can result in your packing on extra pounds. And if you fill up on these things, you may not feel much like eating healthier foods.

Does that mean that you have to give up things with sugar in them? Luckily, no. But instead of gobbling down sugary things every chance you get, you should try to limit them to a treat once in a while. It also helps if you can substitute healthier things that you like  to snack on. A lot of people turn to fruit when they want something sweet. Nuts are another good choice when you need something healthy to munch on.

KNOW WHY YOU'RE EATING AND WHEN TO STOP

Besides eating the right foods, there are some other things that you can do that will help to keep your weight at a healthy level. One of the most important is to learn to stop eating when you are full. Just because you can stuff down more food doesn't mean it's a good idea. Ask yourself, *Is my stomach still hungry or do my taste buds just want more?* If it's your taste buds that are screaming out for more, try saving some of the food for later.

It's also important to understand why you eat. The best reason is because you are hungry. But if you find yourself heading for the refrigerator every time you feel unhappy, remember—eating is only a temporary solution and one that may make you feel worse in the long run. A better idea is to talk to your parents or another adult whom you trust about the things that are bothering you.

GET YOUR BODY MOVING!

Exercise is very important in building a strong, healthy body, so don't forget to get your body moving. You don't have to work out at a gym or become a superjock in order to stay in shape, but you do have to turn off your phone and TV occasionally and move away from your computer every now and then. One of the best exercises is dancing. Walking and riding a bike are two other good ways to keep your weight where it should be. If you would rather do things with a group, why not join a sports team at school or find an activity like hiking that you can do with your friends or your family?

Finally, being healthy is very important; having a perfect body is not. There are very few perfect bodies in the world and getting one usually requires a lot of work. It's far better to spend your time and energy doing things that are more interesting—and more fun.

∽ 10 ∽

CHANGING FRIENDSHIPS

As you may have noticed, your body isn't the only thing that's developing. Your personality, likes and dislikes, and interests often change too as you go through puberty. Of course, that doesn't mean that you're becoming a totally different person. If you've always been on the shy side, you'll probably still be a little that way. But as you get older, you're likely to be meeting new kids and experiencing new things. All this is very exciting! But as a result, friendships that you've had for years sometimes change too.

When you think about it, that shouldn't be surprising. After all, your breasts probably didn't develop exactly the same way as your friends' breasts did, and you may have gotten your period earlier or later than they did. But these differences probably didn't affect your friendships much.

Sometimes, though, other changes happen that make even good friends grow apart. Maybe you've met new girls whom you'd like to hang out with. You still want to do things with an old friend too—just not as much. Things can get complicated if your new friends aren't crazy about your old friend and don't want to include her, or if she doesn't want anything to do with them.

"I still want to be friends with Emma. But I want to be friends with Lori and Sara too, and they think she's really uncool. Why can't I be friends with Emma at home, and Lori and Sara at school? But Emma acts like we still have to be super best friends in middle school just because we were best friends ever since kindergarten. Why can't she make some new friends of her own?"

At other times, the problem may be that you and an old friend aren't changing in the same way or at the same rate.

"We've always been best friends. But now she thinks the things we've always done together are babyish and she doesn't want to do them anymore. We still walk home from school together, but lately she started sitting with other girls at lunch and just ignoring me. What did I do wrong?"

If you're feeling left out when someone you've been best friends with forever seems to be avoiding you, you know it really hurts! But it may surprise you to know that your friend probably feels kind of bad too. Chances are she's unhappy that she may be hurting you but doesn't know how to be friends with both you and her new friends.

What can you do when a close friend doesn't seem to want to be friends anymore—or at least not as much as before? First, keep in mind that this doesn't say anything bad about you. You are still as nice, as much fun to be with, and as good a friend as you've always been. You and your friend are just growing apart, at least for now.

Second, there are probably a number of kids whom you would like who would be happy to be your friend. You just have to give them a chance. It may turn out that you actually have more in common—and more fun—with them than you did with your old friend.

What if you are the one who has grown apart from an old friend? First, the fact that you would rather hang out with your new friends doesn't say anything bad about you, either. Making new friends is part of the fun of growing up. But you will still want to consider your old friend's feelings as much as you can. The problem comes when new friends don't like your old friend and make fun of her, talk about her behind her back, or pressure you not to have anything to do with her at all. In that case, you may want to rethink whether you really want to be friends with these girls.

Finally, just as you and your friend may have grown apart, it sometimes happens that past friends grow back together again when they are older. If that's the case, you will be doubly glad that you were nice to each other now.

Dealing with Mean People

Being popular can seem pretty important to girls going through puberty. It's normal to want to be liked, so it may seem that the more people who think you're really cool, the better. There is nothing wrong with this. The problem comes when some girls are really mean to others who they think aren't as popular. If you are the target of this behavior, it can be hard to know what to do.

"There are these girls in my school who are really pretty, really athletic, and are at the popularity top. They can be really snobby and mean. One of them just came up to me and started yelling right in my face. I had no idea why. She made me feel so much smaller than her, and I'm really tall. But I have some really good friends, and they stood by me."

This girl is smart. She knows that good friends are more important than popular ones. As it happens, she's fairly popular herself. But she's careful to be nice to girls who aren't so lucky.

"There's this part of the cafeteria that's called the reject cafeteria, where the kids who aren't very popular sit. Sometimes I just go in and say something nice to one of them, like 'Hi, I really like your shoes.' You don't have to be friends with everyone, but you can be friendly."

∽ 11 ∾

ROMANTIC FEELINGS

At some point during puberty, you'll probably notice that you're starting to feel differently about boys—or at least certain boys. Until now, boys have been—well, just boys. Some were friends of yours, just like the girls you know who are your friends. Others either paid no attention to you (and you paid none to them), were busy doing boy-things that couldn't interest you less, or were just plain annoying.

But now you may find that you like a particular boy as more than just a friend, and you want him to feel that way about you. Or maybe boys in general seem much more interesting now, and you want them to find you more interesting in return. Many girls develop crushes on movie stars or lead singers in bands. They know that it's very unlikely they will ever meet these guys, but that's okay. It's fun to pretend.

The reason for your increased interest in boys is simple—puberty is preparing you to be able to have adult sexual relationships. And for that to happen, your feelings as well as your body have to change. But, of course, not every girl changes in the same way or at the same time. And since girls enter puberty a year or so earlier than boys, girls often start to develop romantic feelings at a younger age than boys do.

By the way, while many people develop romantic feelings toward members of the opposite sex, you probably already know that some people are attracted to people of the same sex while others are attracted to people of both sexes. But regardless of whether a person is attracted to someone of the same or opposite sex, the romantic feelings experienced are the same.

Romantic and sexual feelings can be very exciting! It's fun to wear a pair of boots that you think make you look kind of sexy, to gossip with other girls about the boys you think are cute, and to have a boy whom you like say he likes you back. But it can also be a very confusing time. What if you couldn't care less about boys? Is there something wrong with you? Don't worry! Not every girl going through puberty becomes obsessed with boys. Just as your boobs develop at a different time and in a different way from another girl's, so do your romantic and sexual feelings. On the other hand, there's nothing wrong with you if you spend a lot of time thinking about a boy (or boys) whom you really like, as long as you don't let it take over your whole life.

But for some girls, all this emphasis on which boys they like and whether boys like them back isn't much fun. Girls going through puberty often feel a lot of pressure to be pretty or sexy so that they will be popular with boys. Those who don't feel attractive may think that boys will never like them or that somehow they aren't worth much. It can be difficult to convince yourself that your looks and your popularity status don't matter when it seems like everyone you know thinks these are the most important things about you.

It you are feeling this way, there are a few things to remember. First, believe it or not, the most important things about you are whether you are a good friend, a kind person, and fun to be with. If that sounds like you, then both boys and girls will want to hang out with you. Eventually, the right special person will come along who thinks you're pretty special too. In the meantime, many kids hang out in mixed groups of boys and girls, so even if some kids are paired off, it doesn't keep you from being part of things. Finally, just be yourself. If you have to pretend to to be someone you're not or do

things you aren't comfortable with to get people to like you, it isn't worth it. After all, you want them to like *you*, not some person you think others want you to be.

SENDING NUDE PHOTOS OF YOURSELF

It may never have occurred to you that a girl would want to send a nude picture of herself to someone else, particularly a boy, but there are several reasons why some girls do this. In many cases, a girl's boyfriend has asked her for a picture of herself with no clothes on. Or perhaps she likes a certain boy and thinks he will like her if she sends him a photo of herself nude, whether he asked for one or not.

Even if you know girls who are doing this and nothing bad has happened to them as a result, there are some things you should keep in mind before you hit "Send." First, the person you send the picture to may not be the only one who will see it. Even if he or she promises to delete your photo, that may not be what happens, and before you know it, your naked body is plastered all over the place. Secondly, once you send it, your photo cannot be unsent. There is no way you can get it back once it has been posted, particularly if it has been passed on to other people, so it may come back to haunt you later.

There are other reasons why texting nude pictures is not a great idea. A girl who sends photos to a boy in the hope that he will like her usually finds that he may like getting the picture, but he doesn't like her any more than he did before.

Other girls may not really want to send naked pictures of themselves but feel pressured to do so. Sometimes the person requesting the photo won't take no for an answer, and the girl finally caves in just to get him

to quit bothering her. In other cases, a girl may worry that her boyfriend will break up with her if she doesn't text him a photo. Occasionally, though, someone asking a girl for a photo may actually threaten her, saying that he will tell on her for something that she did, spread lies about her, or do other things to hurt her. This is a form of sexual harassment and is definitely not okay! (We'll talk more about sexual harassment and what to do about it in the next chapter.)

Remember, your body belongs to you and no one else. If you don't want to share naked pictures of yourself, you don't have to. If a boy really likes you, he will like you whether you send him a nude photo of yourself or not. A good rule is that if you wouldn't want your parents to see the photo, think twice before sending it—because there's always a chance that they will.

∾ 12 ∾

DEALING WITH HARASSMENT

One of the things that can happen now that your body has started developing is that you may attract attention you don't want. Some people may think it's all right to make unwanted sexual comments to you or about you—comments that make you feel bad, uncomfortable, or scared. Sometimes people say these things to your face. At other times they may make sexual comments about you behind your back or over the Internet. It can even be more than words. A person may try to touch your body or pressure you to do something sexual. Someone doing this can be another kid in your school, an adult whom you know, or a total stranger. This kind of bullying is called sexual harassment. And it's important to know what to do when it happens.

"A boy in my school started calling me
Watermelon Tits because I have bigger breasts than
anyone else in my grade. He was always yelling at
me across the playground in front of everyone
and saying, 'Do you want help carrying those
watermelons? I'll be glad to help you.' I tried just
ignoring him, but then he started getting right in my
face, saying, 'Here, I'll help you,' and putting his
hands out like he was going to touch my breasts.
He made me so nervous that I didn't even want to
go to school. Finally, I told my mom and she went
to the principal and demanded that the school do
something to stop him. The principal, my mom, and
his parents had a big meeting, but his father just said,
'What is the problem with a little teasing? It's part of
life, and your daughter should learn to just roll with
the punches.' My mom **lost it** when she heard that!
So did the principal, who said if his son didn't stop
that behavior **immediately**, she would suspend him,
and if that didn't work, she'd have him expelled.
I guess his father didn't want to take that chance,
because he had him transferred to another school."

Sexual harassment isn't just teasing—it's illegal, and
schools have a responsibility to stop it. They can only
do that, however, if they know you're being harassed.

So it's important that you tell your parents and your teachers if this happens. Don't wait, hoping things will get better, because they usually don't. And while you're waiting for the person to stop, you'll be finding it harder and harder to pay attention in class and dreading the next time he or she (because girls can be sexual harassers too) decides to pick on you.

Sexual harassment can come from people you don't know too. It can be even scarier when that person is an adult.

*"I was walking by the drugstore when a man in the parking lot called to me and said, 'If you come over here for a second, I think I have something you'd like to see.' I had a bad feeling, so I started to back away. All of a sudden he stepped out from behind a car and opened his coat. I couldn't believe it! His pants were all unzipped and you could see **everything**! I was really scared, and I started running. As soon as I got home, I called my dad. He called the police, and they found the man and arrested him. Turned out, he'd been doing this to a lot of girls my age."*

This girl was really smart! When she had a bad feeling about the situation, she paid attention to that feeling. She didn't worry about not being "polite," and she didn't let herself be lured closer to the man. *Instead she got out of there as fast as she could!* And she told someone about what had happened as soon as possible so he could be stopped.

Sadly, it sometimes happens that a sexual harasser or a sexual abuser is someone you know—perhaps a friend of your parents, a teacher, a coach, or even a relative. You may have trouble believing that this person actually intends his or her comments or actions to be sexual and that you aren't just mistaking what is happening. This is when it's really important to trust your feelings. If it makes you feel bad, uncomfortable, or afraid, then the person shouldn't be doing it. Ask yourself if you would consider it sexual harassment or abuse if the person were a stranger. If the answer is yes, then it's harassment.

What to Do When You're Harassed

- Tell the person harassing you to stop. He or she may not listen, but it's important that you make it clear that what the person is doing bothers you.

- Let your parents know what is going on and how it makes you feel. Don't wait to say something, hoping things will get better.

- If your parents don't take you seriously (which is *very* unlikely), talk to a teacher, counselor, or another adult you trust and ask for help.

- If you have a bad feeling about a situation you find yourself in, *run away*! If the person tries to stop you, scream your head off!

- Don't let others tell you that you are making a big deal out of nothing or that you should just ignore the person harassing you. *No one* has the right to make sexual comments to you or about you, to touch your body in a sexual way or to make you touch theirs, or to pressure you to do something sexual.

CONGRATULATIONS!

This is a very special time in your life, and you deserve to enjoy it! These pages have been left for you to keep a record of your feelings and thoughts as you go through puberty. You may want to write about the day you got your first period. Or about new things you're learning about yourself. Or maybe even the puberty bummers you're having and how you're solving them. It can even be fun to write about embarrassing things that have happened to you or your friends, so you can laugh about them later. In any event, enjoy these pages—they're for you to use however you wish.

INDEX